Unlock Your Stress Mastery

Staying In Control Of Your Dreams, Business, Health, And Relationships

Connie,

Enjoy the new book for entrepreneurs to master the stress they go through to grow more and sustain that growth over the long term.

Jim Farmer

5/3/2021

Trademarks
ProScan is a registered trademark of PDP, Inc.

Reference List:
PDP, Inc., 2020 Research

*I dedicate this book to Tanya, my beautiful wife – the coach of all coaches.
I am eternally grateful.*

Contents

FOREWORD

It's a Saturday morning in the spring of 2020. Almost the entire world is locked down and socially distanced due to the coronavirus. It's a time future generations will read about in history books.

Me? I'm at home sitting at my deck with Tanya, my wife, and D'ogee, the family dog. It's a picture-perfect scene – the sun is warm and glowing on Tanya's face as she sits opposite me, with a mild mountain breeze cooling the temperature. Behind Tanya are the majestic mountains, piercing the clear blue sky.

Most of the time, I come up here when I'm feeling creative. I grab a cup of coffee and my laptop, and I think (hopefully) great thoughts. But, this Saturday morning was different, and Tanya could see it in my eyes.

"Let's take a hike with the pup. It'll do us good to see something new today. What do you say?" she suggested.

"Can we talk first while I finish my coffee? But yes, a hike sounds great," I replied.

"That's fine. It looks like a hike could do you some good." In her typical loving and healing way, I knew Tanya could see something wasn't right. She knew that the pressures of running a business were causing me stress and distorting the smile on my face.

There's an old tweet that Elon Musk once sent out. The founder of SpaceX and Tesla was talking about the "amazing business life" people think he has, but in reality, it was "great highs, terrible lows, and unrelenting stress. I don't think people want to hear about the last two."

We were definitely experiencing those last two at that moment.

When I started the business, I never had any idea that we would be launching during an economic downturn like this. As a founder, you're at the helm, and there is nobody else you can blame. The buck stops with you.

I knew before I started this business that I would have to deal with stress. My success coach told me stress could either grow you or destroy you. So many entrepreneurs have lost control of their companies and destroyed their wealth, health, and relationships – all because of stress. No one is immune to the pressures that cause stress. But, everyone has control over how they handle it. How you respond to the pressures and demands of life when you start a business depends solely on you.

I understood and appreciated all of what my success coach told me, but this COVID-19 situation was something totally crazy – worldwide, unrelenting uncertainty.

As I sat with Tanya that morning, I put it all out there.

"Should we think about closing the business? Should I go back to corporate life? Could I even land a corporate job during these uncertain times when so many people are losing theirs? How is our business going to survive?"

I even thought about selling our home!

But more importantly, what about the dreams for the business? Our dreams?

Our dream was to have our own business, so I could spend more time with my family – something hard to do when I had a corporate job. If I had to go back to the daily corporate grind, it would destroy all those dreams.

I leaned back in my chair and closed my eyes, feeling the sun on my face. I tried to think positive thoughts. I thought about when we started this business, loving every minute of it because we were providing value to others. We felt empowered, in love with life, free, and grateful. I got to see more of my friends and family. I was genuinely living the dream.

However, those positive thoughts didn't last long. They couldn't. Negativity invaded my mind. I thought about the global crisis, how other people couldn't work, be with family and friends, enjoy going to sporting or social events, grow a business, or be in church to worship with others.

I thought about my own situation. I felt the fear – that I wasn't working, that I was struggling to keep our family's dream alive. I feared for the survival of my business because we were not making sales at the pace we needed to.

Then I thought of my health. Am I going to stay healthy? What about my mom? She's in the hospital.

I was now creating a picture of death in my mind.

Tanya and I began to break this down. We had to choose between holding a picture of abundance (life, growth), or a vision of death (fear, loss). But it's our choice.

We desired a picture of abundance.

Our new startup business serves entrepreneurs by enabling them to live out of abundance to create and live a more efficient, effective, productive life that they love.

In her caring manner, Tanya gave me a loving nudge. "You can have a picture of life, or you can have a picture of fear. The picture you hold and guard in your heart and mind is what will be."

Her wisdom perfectly aligns with why God created us and our search for living the better life.

Tanya was guiding me back to four decades of evidence-based research, and the first principle of quantum physics: consciousness (your mind) creates your life experience.

Found in scripture: As you think, so shall you be. Choose life vs. death. Again, I say choose life vs. death.

She was pointing me to the best possible outcome.

It's amazing how our thoughts translate directly into our biology and shape our life experience. Whatever picture you hold in your mind, your brain translates that picture into chemistry, and places that chemistry in your blood. So, your body will respond to that image in your mind. You can have a picture of love (growth & rebuilding) or a picture of fear (decrease, destroy). Those generate two different chemistries, two different experiences you will have from your response to life's pressures.

At that moment, I had to make that decision to choose love (abundance) over fear (death). What an inflection point!

Once I made that choice, I immediately began to experience, as if it was already happening in the material/physical domain, a more abundant life that begins and ends in the heart and mind. I had taken control of my responses to the pressures of life. I had chosen the right path. I successfully freed my mind of harmful stress. Now I was on a journey to growth and rebuilding.

The choice I made led me to reduce stress, regain control of my life, and find my voice again. It allowed me to level up my confidence and certainty, meaning I could attract more potential, take better action, and amplify results.

Let's put it another way. Now, I'm all-in to build a movement of people whose lives I can serve with value and impact. What's more, I can make this calling a business!

I'm living proof that reducing stress gives you back control over your health. It can save and revive your marriage and repair and grow a family. It can help you scale and sustain your business. Whatever is important to you, reducing stress can help you course-correct and get you where you want.

In case you're still wondering, yes, we did take that hike with D'ogee on that sunny Saturday. On our journey, we replaced the picture of fear with one of abundance in our hearts and minds. We reflected on how it made us feel. I can still feel that power, love, freedom, and gratitude today.

We're living the dream amid stress by managing and reducing harmful stress. Again. And if we can do it, so can you, when you choose love over fear.

Jim Farmer
Co-Founder, FYNS LLC
Author – *Unlock Your Stress Mastery*

INTRODUCTION

"It's not stress that kills us. It is our reaction to it." - Hans Selye

When you sign up to start your own business, you sign up for scalable growth and freedom in work and life, but also you sign up for uncertainty and pressure. Fortunately, that's what entrepreneurs are hard-wired to do – thriving rather than surviving even in times of change and chaos.

I saw a quote recently from Oliver Wendell Holmes Sr.: "Many people die with their music still in them. Too often, it is because they are always getting ready to live. Before they know it, time runs out."

Our studies find that if entrepreneurs are "getting ready to live," where they feel like they are putting their foot on the gas pedal, but the car doesn't go forward, they usually need help to cope with the harmful effects of stress.

This book is here to get you in the most advantageous position possible to stay in control of your stress, so you can realize what's important to you, your dreams, business, health, and relationships.

What's more, we can speed this up for you. What takes decades for some, you can do in mere days. You could learn through trial and error, making mistakes and wasting time – or, you can take a few days to learn from four decades of evidence-based research and more than five million individual case studies of people just like you (PDP, Inc., 2020 Research). You deserve a helping hand – reach out and grab it.

One thing we've discovered in our proven work with the latest scientific and technological advancements is when entrepreneurs can control and self-regulate their responses to the pressures that cause stress, they level up. They build better businesses, serve more value, and live better lives.

I wrote this book to help you do precisely that – to master your response to pressures. When you have this degree of control, pressure doesn't create the type of stress that infiltrates your world. More than five million case studies show that your ability to adapt to pressure-causing stress determines your ability to increase success and fulfillment (PDP, Inc., 2020 Research).

Now, I know what you may be thinking. You think that there are so many books that offer to give you the new "secret" or "formula" to find success and happiness. I've seen them too, and many of these models are useful. However, some of these "prescriptions for success" have something missing. They fail to tell you that to sustain growth in business and life, you need the ability to adapt to the pressures that cause stress.

Unlock Your Stress Mastery has proven "adaptability" baked into the framework, so you'll be able to factor in and reduce stress when pressures arrive, rather than have them reduce you. Negative stress can overthrow you and destroy your wealth, health, and relationships. But it's beatable.

When I've shown people drafts of *Unlock Your Stress Mastery* so they could see what it could do for them, they were amazed to see the ability to have experts write a personal story about them. To see three unique chapters telling their story and having chapters written so accurately based on their input from a quick and simple survey. And seeing the story give more understanding about them than their family or best friend could ever describe. Then having the ability to make it work in their lives by having access to a gold-standard online and on-demand course with group coaching to manage harmful stress that can hold them back from creating the life they want.

At the end of Chapter 3, "Why Must You Manage Stress?" you can take a five-to-ten-minute intuitive ProScan® Survey, whereupon our experts take your survey inputs and ghostwrite three chapters of your personal story. Chapter 1 is you showing up at your best, at the top of your game, enjoying being your most authentic, efficient, effective, and productive self – playing to your strengths and amplifying results. Chapter 2 is where stress is growing you and destroying you (holding you back from realizing what you want in life and work). This chapter is your Private Stress Analysis. Chapter 3 is about how you're coming across to others upon first contact, starting a business, leading a team, managing a project, collaborating on a social event, or delegating activities. This ProScan® Survey has a 96% accuracy rating, based on recent research, case studies, and a field norming of millions of businesspeople. PDP, Inc. spent four decades ensuring top-tier reliability and validity – each of your survey inputs goes into the latest algorithms that compare your response to millions of others in a statistically based study of a cross-section of the working adult population (PDP, Inc., 2020 Research).

We trust you will see why millions of entrepreneurs have already joined the movement to advance in confidence with the initial step of reducing the control that stress has on everybody's work and life.

A peek behind the curtain in Chapter 2 of your personal story: you will see narrative and graphical renderings that show where you are succeeding and failing with stress.

The heavy lifting is on us; all you do is devote five-to-ten-minutes of your time taking a ProScan® Survey. We then write three chapters of your personal story based on your survey inputs, including a Private Stress Analysis.

As promised, a peek behind the curtain, the Private Stress Analysis will give you the following information:

- Where the pressures that cause stress come from – work, social life, family, economic factors, health, and beliefs
- All external and internal forces requiring you to make adjustments to pressures
- Energy drain (emotional, mental, and physical) you're experiencing to deal with stress

- The intensities of good stress and bad stress
- How much energy remains for growth in work and life to:
  - Think better, choose better, and perform better
  - Create the future you want
  - Experience the life you want
  - Feel good about your life
  - Be the best version of yourself
  - Sustain success and fulfillment
  - Level up
  - Commit to something bigger than yourself
  - Serve and deliver value to others
  - Move the needle
  - Amplify impact and profit
  - Live big
  - Love life
  - Do what matters
- The energy that remains to rebuild
  - Repair and bounce back
  - Preventative maintenance to sustain higher levels of productivity, efficiency, and effectiveness
- Your satisfaction index – are you achieving success and seeing rewards for your efforts?
- How stress impacts your decision-making
- How stress is compressing or overextending you

As you can see, the potential of controlling how you react to pressures that cause stress is life-changing. Now, you understand why we want to share our most important tools for unlocking your stress mastery. We want you to realize what is important to you and others and enjoy what you want.

Think of this book as the ultimate meditation for your mind and heart. It will help you spend more time in your strengths, and less time in your weaknesses. You will achieve focus, clarity, effectiveness, efficiency, and influence. Your quest is to strengthen your resolve to keep growing, building your ideal life no matter what pressures the world throws your way. This book is your guide.

As an entrepreneur, what stressful thoughts regularly come into your mind? What keeps you up at night?

- Is it not being able to achieve the results you want in today's landscape?
- Anxiety about the future?
- Worries about hiring and firing?
- Is your team underperforming?
- Do you feel stuck, not making the progress you want?
- Maybe you're no longer a chapter ahead of the market you serve?
- Are you feeding your competition with hard-earned customers?
- Are you feeling overwhelmed?
- Do you procrastinate?

Every business owner faces challenges like these. It's inevitable. And they have to overcome them. It's just part of being an entrepreneur.

But the stressful thoughts – the worries we conjure up in our minds about the unknown – these don't just impact your emotional state, they hinder your path forward. It's up to you to make the decision to take back control of your thoughts, adopt a healthier, more focused mindset, and step into the role you were meant for.

Bad stress inhibits your path to control and grow all aspects of your life. When you're stressed, you're not at your best. And when you're not at your best, it's hard to grow and thrive.

Stress is the biggest reason entrepreneurs lose their focus and energy. Living in stress is living in survival mode. Stress is when your brain and body are knocked out of homeostasis. The stress response is your body's way of trying to return to normal.

Now, all organisms can tolerate stress on a short-term basis. Think about zebras preyed upon and stalked by lions. The moment the zebra senses the threat in their outer environment, they immediately go into survival mode. That's because the zebra switches on their sympathetic nervous system, which mobilizes the entirety of their body's resources, to give them the vital energy to survive. It doesn't go 30%, nor 70% – it goes to 100%.

You're no different. When you begin to turn on that stress reaction, your body and brain get a massive surge of energy – a rush of adrenaline that wakes up your entire being.

How does it happen? I'm sure you've felt it.

The moment you perceive a threat in your outer environment, you turn on your "fight or flight" nervous system. There's a pattern recognition in your thinking brain that signals the part where your sympathetic nervous system is, and you begin to change your normal environment.

The signal goes all the way down to the witless adrenal glands, and all of a sudden, there is a release of adrenaline. This release causes powerful psychological changes in the brain and body:

- Heart rate increases
- Blood pressure increases
- Air passages to the lungs expand
- Respiratory rate increases
- Pupils enlarge
- Blood is redistributed to muscles
- Body's metabolism is altered
- The bodily function of digestion is shut down
- Blood glucose levels are maximized

Now, your body is prepared to do battle. To run, hide, or fight.

The unfortunate thing is too many people become addicted to that adrenaline rush. They put themselves in bondage by needing the people and problems in their lives to reaffirm their addiction to this emotion. They need the complexities, overwhelming feelings, struggles, and bad relationships. They need the problematic situations in their lives because it makes them feel something. They become addicted to a life they don't even like.

But when you're in this survival state, you don't act in desirable ways to grow and develop. What if the threat you perceive isn't a lion or big bad wolf? What if it's your business partner, an employee, or a client? Now you're reacting to the same conditions in your environment because you have had bad experiences in the past with these people. What was once highly adaptive soon becomes maladaptive, because you turn on the stress response, but you can't turn it off in time. Now, you're heading toward losing control of the way you grow and develop.

No organism exists in nature that can live in an emergency or survival mode for an extended length of time. If the zebra were in survival mode for long periods, without finding calm by grazing and enjoying life again, it would eventually die.

If you continue to stay in fear about the uncertainty that causes stress for a prolonged period, you're going to be continually fighting, running away, or putting your life on hold. That's no way to live, love, grow, and develop.

When you are in survival mode, there is not enough energy remaining for growth and rebuilding. Your mental, emotional, and physical energy is drained. You can't think, make decisions, behave, or feel right. You're living in a negative experience of the past, not able to think about creating a better future.

As an entrepreneur, the state of fear inhibits your ability to control yourself and realize your dreams. It moves you away from your business purpose, health, wellbeing, and providing value to others. You can't make the world a better place when you are overcome with fear.

What's more, you actually make yourself sick, as your immune system deregulates and can't do what it needs to do to overcome viruses, cancers, and other foreign agents.

So, sit back, enjoy this book, and take it all to heart. Your life may depend on it.

Chapter 1 – Why Do You Need to Know About Stress?

Entrepreneurs can lose control of their dreams, their business, their health, and their relationships because of the way they adjust to the new pressures put on them.

In This Chapter

- Learn the facts.
- Learn about stress: the invisible epidemic.
- Learn about stress: the most prevalent underlying cause of disease and illness.
- Learn how stress affects us.
- Learn from an entrepreneur's stress story.
- Learn to understand the natural pressure adjustment.
- Learn how the feelings of good stress are entirely different from those of bad stress.
- Learn what stress is.

THE FACTS

A Breakthrough in Assessing Stress

The way we think about stress has changed – thanks to innovations from the world's leading credentialed professionals, research experts, behavioral scientists, cognitive neuroscientists, quantum physics, experienced leaders in business and industry, and the leveraging of the most innovative technology.

We now have a proven scientific survey instrument, ProScan® Survey, that helps you best understand the impact of stress on your life, good and bad.

With agility, the ProScan® Survey speeds up your ability to see all current relevant and significant measurements of stress (including all energy drain levels) that occur when you adjust to pressures from important influences taking priority in your life and causing good and bad stress.

This scientific ProScan® Survey instrument is statistically reliable, based on extensive evidence-based research, case studies, and field norming of over five million businesspeople (PDP, Inc., 2020 Research).

You can now have the confidence to use the ProScan® Survey anytime, anywhere, with anyone, quickly, simply, and accurately.

Because of these spectacular advances, you have the fastest way to identify and measure stress to simply manage and reduce stress's harmful impacts better than ever before.

STRESS: THE INVISIBLE EPIDEMIC

Before we had the ProScan® Survey, experts called stress an invisible epidemic. Scientists had no way to visualize stress – you could not see it even with the world's most powerful microscope. Meanwhile, analysts could not measure stress or report on it.

Trying to manage and reduce stress seemed to be a pointless exercise, and a wave of stress engulfed the world population. We're still feeling the ripple effects of this epidemic today. These repercussions have had such a massive impact on us all. Now more than ever, we need a fast, reliable, and proven method to flatten the stress curve.

STRESS: THE MOST PREVALENT UNDERLYING CAUSE OF DISEASE AND ILLNESS

Ninety percent of all illness and disease is related to stress. It may be hard to believe, but it's true.

The U.S. Federal Government's Centers for Disease Control and Prevention (CDC) shows this figure on its website. Experts at Harvard, Yale, Vanderbilt, the Mayo Clinic, Stanford University, and more agree. If you don't manage and reduce stress, you downgrade the immune system. When this happens, it leads to more than just ulcers and hypertension. You risk mental, emotional, and physical breakdown. It's that simple.

Almost 50% of the U.S. population is currently dealing with chronic illness, such as heart disease, cancer, stroke, diabetes, and obesity. In 2017, 90% of the nation's $3.5 trillion in annual healthcare expenditures was for people with chronic and mental health conditions. This cost is continuing to trend up as of the publication of this book in September 2020.

The leading cause of these chronic and mental health conditions? Unmanaged stress.

As stress levels in the population rise, our healthcare costs are set to climb higher and higher.

HOW STRESS AFFECTS US

Stress is part of the human condition. It's unavoidable. To a certain degree, it's necessary.

Everyone experiences stress every day, in varying forms and amounts.

- In the short term, stress can actually be beneficial. It gives us motivation and helps us focus on the challenges we face. Stress improves our performance. We talk about this type of stress positively when we say that we're "pumped" or "wired."

Problems arise when we let everyday stresses build up.

- In the long term, the excess of stress in our lives surpasses our ability to cope with it. When this happens, stress misdirects our energy rather than focusing it. When we talk about this kind of pressure, we talk about "anxiety," "underperforming," and feeling "burned out."

At this point, we need to find a positive and productive way to manage and reduce stress.

- Many people face similar pressures – work, family, friends, money, health, beliefs – but we all deal with those stress factors differently. The differentiator is a person's perception – someone's perception is their reality. Every person looks at stress through their own lens of understanding, then decides if it's right to adjust to the pressures that cause stress. They evaluate the gain, loss, opportunity, difficulty, stability, uncertainty, security, danger, etc.

Hans Selye, M.D., Professor and Director at the University of Montreal, put it so well:

"Stress is not something to be avoided. The only way to avoid stress would be to do nothing at all. Virtually all human activity involves stress – from a game to a passionate embrace. But this can be defined as the stress of pleasure, challenge, or fulfillment. What we all want is the right kind of stress for the right length of time – at a level that is best for us. Excessive or unvaried stress, particularly frustration, becomes distress. And, this, in turn, can lead to ulcers, hypertension, and mental or physical breakdowns."

Good or bad, stress happens. The trick is keeping it on the right side of the line.

In this table, you'll see that the first column shows the outcomes of having the right kind of stress for the proper length of time – at a level that is best for you. The second column shows what happens when your stress is excessive, prolonged, or repetitive.

Figure 1.1   Stress Outcomes

Good Stress	Bad Stress
Enhances relationships	Destroys relationships
Operates out of intimacy, passion for life, and love for others	Operates out of isolation and fear of loss
Results in growth, fulfillment, satisfaction, peace, happiness, joy, clarity, self-esteem, and generosity	Causes decline, failure, dissatisfaction, anger, depression, confusion, self-shame, selfishness, worthlessness, and frustration
Energizing, low energy drain	Tiring, high energy drain
Directs energy correctly	Misdirects energy
Boosts the immune system	Suppresses the immune system
Lowers blood pressure	Raises blood pressure
Stimulates emotional, mental, physical, and behavioral growth	Deters emotional, mental, physical, and behavioral growth
Keeps us healthy	Makes us sick
Promotes better nutrition and metabolism	Causes bad eating and metabolic disorders
Fosters good thoughts	Generates bad thoughts
Stimulates creativity and higher neurological activity	Destroys and dumbs down
Counteracts addiction and withdrawal	Increases addiction
Promotes faster healing	Depresses healing
Increases trust and enables better decision-making	Causes distrust and bad judgment
Opens cells to healing and regeneration	Closes cells and leads to emotional, physical, mental, and behavioral Breakdowns

Research shows that bad stress literally switches on an alarm system in your brain that leads to a release of hormones. These hormones, adrenaline, and cortisol result in the signs and symptoms shown in the second column.

Your body is naturally hard-wired to react to pressures. It goes back to the days when we had to protect ourselves against predators. Sure, such threats are rare today, but we have developed our own risks that we need to defend ourselves against.

Think of common pressures we all face. It could be:
- Completing your education
- Achieving goals
- Balancing work and life
- Securing finances
- Overcoming conflicts
- Getting a job
- Earning a promotion
- Leading a team
- Completing projects on time and on budget
- Starting a business
- Growing a business
- Raising children
- Taking care of family
- Planning for the future

Your body treats all of these as pressures. As a result, you may always feel like there's a heavy weight on your shoulders. But, you can manage and reduce stress. You don't have to let stress rule your life.

Think of the pressures you face as an entrepreneur. I'm sure you will see some of yourself in Andy's story.

AN ENTREPRENEUR'S STRESS STORY

With his contagious energy and passion, Andy founded a company called HanHol Medical.

HanHol revolutionized the way doctors access patients' bedside monitors, whether the doctor is inside the hospital, at home, in a care facility, or anywhere else. Andy's company gave doctors a way to see all patient bedside monitors on their mobile devices – anytime, from anywhere. It meant that doctors could virtually step inside the patient's room and be at any patient's bedside to make more accurate clinical decisions faster, enabling rapid responses to their patients' healthcare needs.

Andy drove his startup to become one of the fastest-growing mobile technology companies in the healthcare space. The company's solution saved thousands of lives and saved each hospital system millions of dollars every year.

By creating a better patient experience, lowering healthcare costs, and saving lives, Andy's startup company of 25-strong employees built momentum, impact, and profit. The success of HanHol was unprecedented. That success came with great highs, significant lows, and pressures.

Before starting HanHol, Andy connected with me for coaching to confirm that his natural strengths were in an entrepreneur's sweet spot. I administered the ProScan® Survey to give Andy his answer. And within five minutes, he had what he wanted and needed.

When I first met Andy, he was a practicing physician, dreaming of running a company. Using the ProScan® Survey, we confirmed his natural entrepreneurial strengths and saw why he was frequently frustrated as a practicing physician. With that, Andy decided to exit the medical practice and take the risk to launch an innovative new company. He shifted his focus to creating a new future, something bigger than himself, something that excited him daily, something he would be all-in with, putting his passion out there, and receiving the life he loved by contributing value to others.

When he began to see the decision's impact, he imagined rewriting the healthcare playbook to save lives and money through better healthcare, and Andy felt alive. He finally found that he was being and doing, through the power of his mind and heart, what once was only a dream.

Through coaching, Andy found that entrepreneurs (as our four decades of work have proven are naturals at:

- Imagining and creating new solutions
- Using their imagination to see what others cannot easily see
- Seeing things before other people see it
- Going straight for the outcome
- Not becoming enamored with processes, systems, or rules
- Making processes, systems, and rules serve them and others
- Finding the shortest way to where an innovation transforms from a thought in the mind and desire of the heart into part of the physical realm
- Creating game-changing products that deliver value and impact to people
- Out-innovating corporate behemoths, always being a chapter ahead of the market, getting better results by being nimble
- Going all-in to make it happen
- Taking risks now in expectation of a future payoff (not in the form of a traditional corporate paycheck)

Andy was confident. His ProScan® Survey results communicated, for the first time in his life, his true authentic self. He said this is a secret revealed in self-education and, through his research, found that most of the world's greatest leaders found this through their self-education and development.

Andy had a lot of credentials to his name, but he also believed what the great American entrepreneur Jim Rohn said: "Formal education will make you a living; self-education will make you a fortune." He had far more of a connection with the things he had learned through self-education than any of his degrees. Andy's professional coaches and mentors taught from experience, as opposed to professors who explained what they had yet to do in the real world.

During the launch of his new company, and the subsequent two years of rapid growth, Andy encountered stress. However, his initial Private Stress Analysis indicated that it was the good, positive stress, and Andy agreed. Andy was managing the pressures, as he was in a role that allowed him the freedom to be his entrepreneurial self.

Good stress is the spice of life – short-term stress relevant to bringing the pleasure of challenge and fulfillment. It is stress with minimal energy drain. It brings epiphanies, clarity, focus, and improved performance. It made Andy feel empowered, free, alive, and grateful. Compared to bad stress that drains your energy and makes you angry, frustrated, and afraid, good stress is what gets you up in the morning, relishing the challenge.

During this time, Andy was operating as the Founder and CEO of HanHol, showing up as the best possible version of himself.

Andy loved the fact that his ProScan® Survey results showed him that he was operating out of his most effective, efficient, and productive natural self. He was thrilled playing to his natural entrepreneurial strengths, in an environment that gave him the freedom to do so. Andy's natural entrepreneurial strengths moved the needle of impact and profit, contributing value to others, making the world a better place. When you do what you love and find sustainable success in doing it, energy flows.

What the ProScan® Survey results proved to Andy is that when you feel good, you do good. When you're playing to the best version of yourself, you contribute your best. As this continues, you create a virtuous cycle – you feel great and do better work, which makes you feel even better, which makes you…play from your strengths and realize your full potential.

Here are some excerpts from Andy's best version of himself:

- Convincingly authoritative and action-oriented. A doer and driver to get results that may be somewhat unconventional. Very competitive and goal-directed, usually within an organizational setting not bound by "this is the way it's always been done."
- Appreciates systematic structure in realizing speed-to-innovating, speed-to-results, speed-to-development, and more raving fans (clients) than the competition, delegates details to teams and others, and requires accurate results.

- Effective in developing people to enable them to do what they love and do it well; at the same time, very direct and independent. Enjoys social interaction. Comes across more strongly than he realizes.
- He is self-confident, controlling, aggressive, competitive, direct, results-oriented, and a calculated risk-taker.
- Exhibits a daring fearlessness with a do-or-die determination. He has a need for total control to make the company perform to create a better world for others.
- Big-hearted, friendly, empathetic, interactive, and interested in people. Loves socializing, and team interaction is natural.
- He is found to be a non-traditional, candid, informal, and general (big picture – solution-oriented) person. Known for being independent and a free-thinker, prefers to delegate matters of a technical and detailed nature to others unless a strong sense of motivation exists.
- Is a fast-paced, action-oriented, and impatient person. He is a doer and driver, and perhaps seeks change for the better.

Andy was stoked about the journey he was on. However, things changed – as they always do.

It all changed after HanHol's board voted for Series C funding, and massive amounts of money came into the company, all with the focus on scaling. The aim was to go from rapid growth to what they called hypergrowth.

This meant venture capitalists gaining more influence and control. Within a few weeks, there were new people on the board of directors, a new COO, and other significant changes to the company's leadership team.

Then, suddenly, Andy's role was demoted from Founder and Chief Executive Officer to Founder and Chief Innovation Officer.

Two months later, I got a call. It was Andy. "I'm calling you because the business has stopped feeling like fun," he said.

Andy asked to take the Private Stress Analysis to see if the analysis could measure why he was now going through the motions of life and living on autopilot, losing energy, and getting stuck in doubt and division.

Andy wanted more clarity and focus. He wanted to contribute in a way that he lived, loved, and mattered. The environment Andy was now in did not align with that.

He stated, "Let's put the Private Stress Analysis to the test and clarify the measurable impacts of all this harmful negative stress. The last time I took the stress analysis, it nailed how stress brought pleasure, challenge, and fulfillment. However, that's not what's happening now."

Andy was all-in. He knew from my coaching when he started the business – what you don't measure, you don't manage. And what you don't manage, you don't change. Andy valued that coaching, as he told me, "I need clarity to change for the better."

He took out his mobile phone, logged in, and within ten minutes, he had completed the ProScan® Survey and received the results.

We then arranged a fifteen-minute talk to review the results, as well as a sixty-minute coaching session for later – all via Zoom.

When Andy showed up at the Zoom meeting, he had this look of amazement on his face. "Wow!" he said. "I mean, WOW! It's like you know me better than my family or my best friend! How did this ProScan® Survey generate so much knowledge in so little time? In the ten minutes it took me to take the survey, you turned weeks of analysis into minutes while making it more reliable, valid, relevant, and vital. And, it's so freaking simple. It's dialed me in and shown me the measurements of how I've been adjusting to outside pressures and shown me their effects. It's giving me the ability to unlock my mastery of stress. Now, I can reduce my stress and get control again – control of my dreams, my business, my health, and my relationships."

Let's peek behind the curtain of Andy's Private Stress Analysis. The following is just a snapshot of the outtakes, giving you a feel of how harmful stress was robbing Andy of control and a better life.

Abbreviated Excerpts of Andy's Private Stress Analysis

Stress

- You are feeling restricted or limited from utilizing your natural potential at work.
- Energy Drain is significant and causes concern as focus and energy are not currently available for growth and rebuilding.
- Over-expectations are diminishing true satisfaction as more is expected of you than you feel comfortable in delivering.
- Current expectations demanded of you do not align with you being at your most efficient, effective, and productive self.

Adjustments to pressures

- Stepping back and not being as forceful, innovative, creative, and assertive as would be natural.
- Being less communicative, quieter. The result is from a change in roles that requires a more objective and direct approach with people.
- Let down, disappointed, and not appreciated.
- Realizing things are not going to happen as quickly as preferred; thus waiting for others, or not pushing as hard as would be natural.
- Over-engineering causing the feeling of being overwhelmed and procrastination.
- Gathering specific factual information to validate making a change.

Low Satisfaction

- Concern as to whether or not goals and aspirations are being met.
- Not receiving relevant and current rewards for efforts put forth.
- A sense of discouragement, dissatisfaction.
- Indicates stress is negative (harmful).

After seeing the stress analysis and sitting down with me for coaching, Andy clearly understood what he needed to do. He would exit the company on his terms, play to his strengths, spend less time in what steals his energy, and do the things that matter most with focus, clarity, and better energy. Amazing what clarity will do.

Fast forward. Today, Andy innovates and creates, launches and grows new companies, then sells them to giant behemoths to broaden the value to others. Andy spends more time with his family for their wellbeing, connecting himself to what is bigger than himself – philanthropy and charity. He enjoys working wherever he wants in the world while making more money than he did as HanHol's Chief Innovation Officer.

Andy loves his life. He loves the new freedom. He loves the legacy he is creating for others to benefit from.

And all because he took the opportunity to measure stress in order to manage, take control of, and reduce harmful stress and create a new future that gives him the freedom to be his best to give his best.

UNDERSTANDING THE NATURAL PRESSURE ADJUSTMENT

When you encounter a perceived threat, such as a car heading straight towards you, your hypothalamus (a small region located at the base of the brain, about the size of a pearl) sounds the alarm system in your body.

This part of your brain functions like a command center, communicating with the rest of your body via the nervous system, giving you the energy to fight or flee. Through a combination of nerve and hormonal signals, the system prompts your adrenal glands, located on top of your kidneys, to release a surge of hormones, including adrenaline and cortisol.

Adrenaline increases your heart rate, raises your blood pressure, and boosts energy supplies. Cortisol, on the other hand, is the primary stress hormone. It increases glucose in your bloodstream, enhances your brain's use of glucose, and increases the availability of the substance that enables the preliminary repairs of tissues.

Cortisol also curbs functions that are non-essential or even detrimental in a fight-or-flight situation. It changes responses in your immune system and suppresses the digestive system, the reproductive system, and growth processes. It also affects the areas of your brain that control mood, motivation, and fear.

So, when your brain is faced with these situations on an excessive scale, for a prolonged length of time, or repeatedly, your natural adjustment system goes haywire.

Usually, this process is self-limiting. Once a perceived threat has passed, your hormone levels return to normal. Adrenaline and cortisol levels drop, your heart rate and blood pressure return to where they should be, and other systems return to their regular activities.

However, when you're always under stress, and you constantly feel under attack, that natural fight-or-flight adjustment never turns off.

When this happens on a long-term basis, it can disrupt almost all of your body's processes. This is what puts you at an increased risk of severe problems, including:

Cognitive
- Memory problems
- Inability to concentrate
- "Brain Fog"
- Excessive negative thoughts
- Poor judgment
- Anxiety
- Indecision
- Constant worrying
- Starting many tasks, but completing few
- Self-doubt

Emotional
- Moodiness
- Depression

- Irritability
- Agitation
- Feeling overwhelmed
- Unable to relax
- Sense of isolation
- Loneliness
- Fatalistic thinking
- Panic
- Cynicism
- Anxiety
- Frustration

Physical

- Constipation
- Nausea
- Headaches
- Dizziness
- Loss of sex drive
- Chest pain
- Rapid heartbeat
- Aches and pains
- Chronic illness
- Skin complaints
- Indigestion
- High blood pressure

Behavioral

- Social isolation
- Loss of sense of humor
- Procrastination
- Alcohol and drug abuse
- Neglecting responsibilities
- Unaccountability
- Compulsive behaviors
- Lack of appetite
- Insomnia

- Oversleeping
- Feeling demotivated

Unfortunately, in today's uncertain chaotic world and all the changes and pressure that come with it, most of the population finds itself in a constant, chronic state of fight or flight. Our adrenals are repeatedly pumping out cortisol and adrenaline and other stress hormones, overloading our bodies. These hormones tell our bodies to shut down all but the essential survival systems, to prepare for the speed and volume of the threats at hand.

When we are in this state for prolonged periods, our emotional, mental, physical, and spiritual states barely have a chance to rest or repair. Without adjusting to growth-and-rebuilding mode, a person shows the symptoms displayed in the second column of the Good Stress and Bad Stress table. See Figure 1.1 Stress Outcomes, in Chapter 1.

Unmanaged, bad stress becomes a killer.

Here's what you need to do: check in with yourself to identify the type of stress you are feeling, whether it's good or bad stress. Is tension draining your energy? Do you feel like the world is boxing you in? Are you extending yourself beyond what you feel comfortable in delivering? Is stress robbing you of life's enjoyment and satisfaction?

If the answers are yes, it's time to take action.

Good or bad, stress happens. You have the opportunity to manage it better, and reduce the harmful effects of stress in your life, before it manages and reduces you.

THE FEELINGS OF GOOD STRESS ARE ENTIRELY DIFFERENT FROM THOSE OF BAD STRESS

Good stress releases an entirely different hormone and other peptides in the brain.

Research shows that people living with good stress – the right kind of stress for the proper length of time – at a level appropriate for them have healthy levels of oxytocin and other peptides in the brain and hormonal system. Oxytocin is often called the "love hormone!"

Our evidence-based research indicates that self-aware people release higher levels of oxytocin. It's a desirable trait to be aware of your natural strengths – who you are and the benefits you can bring to yourself and others. With self-awareness like this, you're in a prime position to manage and reduce your stress.

As a result, you better leverage your strengths, maintaining the right kind of stress for the right amount of time, at the right level for you. It sets you up for a fulfilling life, with intimate relationships, friends, and community. You are ready to achieve fuller potential in life, to build a better world and think creatively. You're healthy and happy.

When you're happy with yourself, it activates the part of your brain that makes you feel pleasure, as well as releasing oxytocin. The higher your oxytocin levels, the more generous you are to yourself and others.

You're experiencing what it's like to live in the first column of the Good Stress and Bad Stress table. See Figure 1.1 Stress Outcomes, in Chapter 1. To put it simply, you're living the good life.

WHAT IS STRESS?

Everybody experiences stress. We talk about it incessantly. We feel its effects, such as energy drain. But what actually is it? What is stress?

Stress is the energy drain you experience when you adjust to any pressure put upon you.

It doesn't matter what the pressure is. It doesn't matter what the impact is (positive or negative). Stress is the measurable energy drain that results from your efforts to adjust to any pressure for change.

Being able to define stress in this way creates a breakthrough in stress management. When we can measure the energy drain that we have at a given moment relevant to stress, we can manage stress. Why manage stress? So you can reduce the harmful destruction negative stress has on your dreams, health, wealth, and relationships.

The benefits of being able to measure stress are immense. On average, adjusting to pressures can quickly drain 25-50% of your potential energy. Plus, we know how bad stress can increase that energy drain to the point of destroying your wealth, relationships, and health (cause chronic illness) if left unmanaged.

Quite simply, being able to measure stress will help us realize the toll stress is taking on our lives and the lives of others.

Chapter 2 – What Must You Understand About Stress?

Stress can grow you or destroy you.

In This Chapter

- Learn how stress can creep up on you.
- Learn what drains your energy.
- Learn how pressures come from priority environments.
- Learn the good and bad of stress.

As an entrepreneur, it's not just your stress you have to manage. You need to look after your people's stress levels too.

In XYZ Inc., they all work remotely, so management must have simple ways to stay on top of managing and leading people, and keep complex pressures from causing harmful stress. You can't wait until it is too late.

HOW STRESS CAN CREEP UP ON YOU

Let me tell you a story about Mary, one of the salespeople in XYZ Inc. Mary was what you'd describe as a top-tier salesperson. She was competitive and demanded a great deal from herself and others. She exhibited the strengths of problem-solving and taking charge. She was confident, direct, results-oriented, decisive, persuasive, and authoritative. Each year, Mary exceeded sales expectations for the three-year-old startup company. The founder of the 37 employee-based startup loved Mary – wanting her to stick around and planning to model and hire more salespeople like her. Mary brought in 45% of the company sales, with another sales rep bringing in 30%, and a third bringing in 25%. The company was exceeding sales targets each year, taking the company to higher levels of success.

Life was good at XYZ Inc. Sales and marketing activities were turning into healthy profits. The company's speed of understanding its customers' problems and delivering results had set it on an extraordinary growth trajectory.

Then suddenly, things changed.

For the first time, Mary's sales began to slump at XYZ Inc.

I received a Zoom meeting invite from the founder. You could feel the concern and urgency in his voice. He heard about my coaching work from his best friend, with whom I had worked through entrepreneurship stresses to level up success over the long term. The founder was ready to engage us to coach Mary, his top salesperson. He intuitively knew he needed Mary back in the sales game to bust the company out of a sales slump and fuel and sustain growth. It was clear that it would take something more than sales training. He knew Mary was the best of the best with a proven extraordinary record of success; look at what she had already achieved here. She had an impeccable track record of creating profitable growth across the previous three startups. He could see it had nothing to do with her high-performance sales habits. Something was limiting her ability to play full out. She was not at the top of her game, no longer leveraging her strengths.

Three weeks later...

Mary called me to change her weekly Zoom coaching to a face-to-face session. She told me that it was about the company granting her a stock option last month, and she needed to flesh something out.

I drove over to Mary's house, and as soon as I arrived, I could see that she was not her usual confident self.

We sat down around her large glass desk. We were looking at the ocean from Mary's home office window, eye level with the surf and the sunset reflecting on the ocean waves. What a breathtaking view.

I asked her straight up, "Why are you so panicked about this stock offer?"

Mary leaned back in her chair and gazed out at the ocean view. Sitting quietly and staring off into space was not like Mary at all.

I knew she valued coaching, so I asked her the question again.

Finally, she looked at me and started to speak: "I think I'm going to…"

I leaned in, and our eyes met. I didn't need to say a word.

Mary slowly raised her hand to cover her magnetic blue eyes as a single tear found its way down her face. She discreetly wiped the tear away in hopes that I didn't notice. She knew she couldn't keep the breaking story within.

"Okay," Mary said. "With the offer, I thought I would be a lot further along than I am. I'm scared of getting the sales back up and going."

"Why?" I replied.

"Because I'm fearful of letting our founder and investors down. I've been leading with record-breaking sales for three years while forgoing sleep, friendships, family relationships, exercise, and good nutrition for this startup. However, I'm experiencing anxiety, self-doubt, depression, and loneliness. And, it's cascading into the relationship with my husband and kids. My daughter asked me why I spend so little time with her. My son is only seeing his father at his football playoffs, asking where Mom is. My best friend let me know that she feels our relationship is too one-sided. All of this is in the not-so-good column. Plus, totally unexpected, I had what I thought was a heart attack last week while on a date with my husband. The date ended up in the emergency room, thank God it was a false heart attack. The next morning I had a follow-up visit with my primary care physician, where he referred me to a stress management specialist. I didn't sign up for this. I'm so drained."

As a coach, I've worked with many people like Mary – high performers who fight long and hard for success, on a journey of startup-above-all-else approach. And then, they incoherently step into stress that takes them out of their game, where they experience the feeling of being overwhelmed, plateauing, or freezing up. To others, they may appear confident and in control as they strive to level up. However, they often feel rising pressure internally and externally. I call it the death of the high performer. Our research proves that it's a leading cause of top performers not creating and living, loving, and having a better life.

Put simply, unmanaged stress destroys the ability to control your life. If the high performer doesn't adjust to the pressures in a healthy way, stress takes its course, leading to chronic stress, which wreaks havoc on the high performer's physical, mental, emotional, and spiritual health. And at this point, they're entering the slippery slope where stress inhibits the high performer's ability to be the best version of themselves.

Then, more pressure comes when they try to replicate or scale their previous success. Relevant rewards and satisfaction are missing for doing what they're doing. They feel overextended – too many expectations with too much already on their plate. Or, compressed – squeezed or boxed in, not experiencing a fuller potential.

They've come so far in life but never developed techniques for better managing stress. Even though they're competent, they live in fear that they will fail to handle the demands which come with leveling up success. If the picture of fear develops in the high performer's mind, they downgrade their ability to better self-regulate, generate wealth, and maintain healthy relationships.

On the other hand, how do some people break free and keep rising higher, experiencing fulfillment, wellbeing, abundance, and long-term success that seem unreachable to others?

This book is all about how people better deal with stress. It gives clear and proven direction, and explains why some excel, others fail, and far too many never try to manage their anxiety and the harmful impact stress has on their entire lives. After all, you can't level up, move the needle, impact, profit, and continue to provide value to others if overwhelmed by stress.

Back to Mary...

Mary completed the Stress Mastery Course and coaching in days versus weeks. As a result, Mary is crushing it with energy, impacting, and profiting as the top salesperson. She spends more time with her husband and kids, takes vacations, and is back into training for a marathon with her friend.

As you read this book, it will show you how to understand stress. To see good stress, which will grow you, and the bad stress that will destroy you. It will guide you to grow and rebuild your quality of life by managing and reducing harmful stress.

Are you ready?

WHAT DRAINS YOUR ENERGY?

Adjusting to external or internal pressures put upon you drains your energy. The energy we are referring to is emotional, mental, and physical.

But what kind of pressures? Let's look in more detail.

PRESSURES COME FROM PRIORITY ENVIRONMENTS

Everybody faces pressures in their lives. No one is immune to having pressures placed upon them. Where do these pressures come from?

Pressures that drain your energy originate from critical environments that take priority in your life right now. These priority environments are the major areas of your life where you live and work to bring value to yourself and others.

You will recall in Part 2 of the ProScan® Survey, you responded to "How you feel others expect you to be or act," which triggered your lightning-fast mind to remember what actions you believe others expect of you. This part of the survey triggered thoughts from the past four to eight weeks, relating to your life's current, relevant, and significant environments.

Each of your 60 survey inputs went through our validated algorithms. It compared your responses to others who answered similarly in a statistically based study of a cross-section of the working adult population. We precisely identify and bring clarity to the pressures you face; we measure the energy you use to adjust to each pressure. The ProScan® Survey is a one-of-a-kind study – no one has done anything like this before.

However, only you know the specific people and circumstances that cause the pressures that require you to adjust. Our certified coaches help guide and speed up identifying the people and situations to remove ambiguity.

When you measure the pressures from influences that take priority in your life, causing you to feel the need to make adjustments, you become better at managing the energy drain and regaining control to realize a healthy outcome.

For all of us, pressures will come from one (or more) of these six significant environments:
- Work
- Social life

- Family
- Economic factors
- Health
- Beliefs

THE GOOD AND BAD OF STRESS

Together, we have learned that:

- The definition of stress is energy drain
- Stress and energy drain come from adjusting to pressures
- Pressures come from people and circumstances in one or more of six environments, relevant to you at that specific time

Now, let's do a deeper dive into the good and bad stress we referred to earlier.

In daily life, when we use the term "stress," we are usually describing negative situations.

This leads many to believe that all stress (or energy drain) is terrible for you. This is not true.

Stress has two forms – eustress and distress.

Eustress refers to positive stress, while distress means negative stress. There is a difference.

Let's look at these terms in more detail.

Eustress is a positive outcome from energy drain. It has the following characteristics:
- Motivates and focuses energy
- Short term
- Minimal energy drain
- Within your coping abilities
- Feels exciting
- Improves performance
- Brings average or high satisfaction

In contrast, distress, or negative stress, is an adverse outcome from excessive, prolonged, or repetitive energy drain. It has these characteristics:

- Causes anxiety or concern, and misdirects energy
- Can be short or long term
- Higher energy drain
- Perceived as outside your coping abilities
- Feels unpleasant
- Decreases performance
- Brings low satisfaction

Chapter 3 – Why Must You Manage Stress?

Stress management techniques can grow and rebuild your wealth, health, and relationships.

In This Chapter

- Learn why pressures can make or break you as an entrepreneur.
- Learn from Mike's story – how stress builds up and takes control of an extraordinary high performer.
- Learn how to set your foundation for managing stress.
- Learn about the "Stress Mastery Course" – manage stress and control your dreams, business, health, and relationships.
- Learn the three keys to managing stress – unlocking your stress mastery.

WHY PRESSURES CAN MAKE OR BREAK YOU AS AN ENTREPRENEUR

Why do certain entrepreneurs succeed while others fail in dealing with pressures and demands? What is the key for an entrepreneur to overcome these forces to live a life of achievement and fulfillment?

Entrepreneurs ask these questions frequently. That started our journey – researching the world's happiest and most successful entrepreneurs and teams that succeed more quickly than others and sustain their success over the long term.

We set out to confirm evidence that entrepreneurs who apply personal and professional development to learn to manage stress elevate achievement and fulfillment in their life and work.

For context, let's define managing stress. Let's decode the meaning of both words – managing and stress. Managing is to self-regulate to handle, direct, govern, or control in action or use. Stress, decoded in Chapter 1, is the measurable energy drain resulting from your efforts to adjust to any pressure for change.

So, what is our definition of managing stress? Managing stress is to self-regulate a healthy adjustment to any pressure for change made on you. Why is this so essential? Self-regulating a healthy adjustment to any pressure for change frees you, the entrepreneur, from living like a captive to pressures. This is you as an entrepreneur using stress as a positive force to achieve a rewarding lifestyle.

Now that we have our definition, let's get back to the research.

To advance our research, we took a cross-section of entrepreneurs faced with the same set of intense pressures and demands, operating in the same industry, and serving solutions to the same market to solve the same problems.

Then we divided the entrepreneurs into two groups relevant to their mindsets. The first group applied personal and professional development to learn to manage stress. And the second group avoided taking personal and professional development to learn to manage stress.

Fast forward to the research findings.

The entrepreneurs who leveled up their ability to learn to better adjust to pressures freed themselves from unhealthy stress limitations. Outcome: growth and rebuilding in chaotic high-pressure times. These entrepreneurs enjoyed higher satisfaction and wealth (emotional, mental, and physical), faster business success, and sustainable business success.

The entrepreneurs who avoided leveling up their ability to learn to better adjust to pressures ended up constraining themselves with unhealthy stress limitations. Outcome: death and breakdown in chaotic high-pressure times. These entrepreneurs had lower satisfaction and wealth (emotional, mental, and physical), less business success, and unsustainable business success.

The answer to the entrepreneur's questions?

Successful entrepreneurs who apply personal and professional development to learn to manage stress elevate achievement and fulfillment for a better life.

As we continue with research, listening, learning, and growing, we confirm when entrepreneurs avoid managing stress, it builds up more stress. And with more stress comes more limitations that downgrade the entrepreneur's ability to self-regulate, grow, and rebuild, especially during chaotic uncertain times.

These limitations wreak havoc on their daily lives. They begin to experience breakdowns in creative energy flow, control, influence, meeting deadlines, attention to detail, and decision-making—the limitations then cascade into lower-level emotions where the entrepreneur begins to operate out of anger, fear, uncertainty, and doubt. And if stress goes unmanaged for extended periods, the entrepreneur declines in their beliefs, certainty, potential, actions, and results. This tees up for more pressure because the entrepreneur finds it much harder to think better, choose better, act better, experience better, and feel better.

Substantial evidence underscores the proof that entrepreneurs face multiple stressors that can diminish their happiness and success if stress remains unmanaged. Ninety percent of all limitations for the entrepreneur to realize goals and aspirations are related to stress.

The good news is when entrepreneurs manage stress, they control what's important to themselves, the ones they love, and the customers they serve. All our evidence-based research findings indicate this as truth.

So, we set the bar high using top-tier research standards and best practices, so all measurements of the impact of stress on anyone can be precisely measured to help them change for the better.

As we learned in earlier chapters, what the entrepreneur better measures, the entrepreneur better manages. And what the entrepreneur better manages, the entrepreneur better changes.

Before unpacking the keys to unlock your stress mastery, Mike's story is available to answer a frequently asked question: "Why Must You Manage Stress?" The story shows you how stress and anxiety build up and takes control of an extraordinary high performer.

After you read Mike's story, learn about the three keys to unlocking your stress mastery and join the movement to continue your journey to control scalable growth and rebuilding for your health, wealth, and relationships. Don't know how to start?

Learn more at the end of the chapter on how our Stress Mastery Course is the perfect course to reprogram your "Success Switch."

MIKE'S STORY – HOW STRESS BUILDS UP AND TAKES CONTROL OF AN EXTRAORDINARY HIGH PERFORMER

Mike is an extraordinary high performer game-changer entrepreneur at Tenterdon's Inc. He's also a highly sought-after leader in the social media space. He's the life of the party; he's encouraging and inspiring. He's one of those people you just feel great being with.

However, in the last month, Mike has not been his usual self. And last Tuesday, when we had our monthly coaching, his behavior was totally out of the ordinary.

For starters, Mike was a few minutes late, arriving just after 7 am. Typically, he's in the office at 6:30 am sharp. He looked tired. He was not his warm, friendly, and empathetic self.

Even though we were starting late, we headed over to the break room for our traditional caffeine fix – triple-shot espressos. Then, we went to Mike's office. The office is an array of the latest and greatest gadgets known to humanity and monitors are suspended from everywhere you can imagine. It's like NASA command center in there!

Mike sat down and quickly scanned his messages. It wasn't a pretty sight:

- He did not respond to a message from Jane a couple of days ago for approving the marketing budget.
- He gave Ron the wrong configuration for the new wearable device design.
- There was a story about a competitor on Instagram, causing a distraction.
- Plus, a notification on Slack telling Mike his creative team did not receive his input last week to prioritize the social media targeting ads.
- His marketing executive was finding that Mike dropped the ball on the rollout plan for the social media campaigns due by noon today.

Mike turned to me and said, "Have you ever felt like you put your foot on the gas pedal, but the car doesn't go forward?"

Mike just seemed to be doing a lot of things lately, only to spin his wheels and not really accomplish anything. At the same time, he joined an online meeting with an executive team halfway around the world and felt so overwhelmed that he couldn't find his presentation he put together last night for this very moment!

I saw his knee beginning to bounce up and down like a basketball. He intermittently bit his lip and reached for his triple-shot espresso in an attempt to shake off that tired and dumbed-down feeling.

With panic in his eyes and frustration in his voice, he demanded that I get his admin to immediately bring us two more espressos. This was totally out of character.

I could see that he was trying so hard to recall the main points of the presentation that he couldn't think creatively enough to communicate persuasively to everyone else in the online meeting. The meeting, where he was supposed to get the executive team's buy-in to advance the new platform concept to the design and prototype team, was a disaster.

Then, Mike lost concentration again, when his calendar alerted him to another long-forgotten yet essential meeting on Friday. Wow, and it was only 8:30 am, when would this day end?

Clearly, Mike was not himself and hadn't been for a while. I was not the only one who had noticed either. I knew that Mike's wife took Jack's wife aside during the company party last weekend to tearfully tell her how worried she was about her husband.

"What happened to Mike, the life of the party? He's irritable with the kids and me. He tosses and turns all night in bed. He's tired all the time – emotionally and mentally. He can't focus on anything. Also, he's been to the cardiologist for a heart screening, even though he works out three times a week. What are we going to do?"

How many of us have heard a story like this before? How many know someone like Mike – someone we live, work, or play with occasionally or frequently? How many of us feel like this?

If you do, you're not alone.

The thing is, Mike is heading towards a downward spiral at home and work if he does not manage and reduce his stress.

It is not too late, and the earlier Mike identifies and determines where the stress is coming from, the better he can manage it. The quicker Mike acts, the better it is for himself, his wife, and his children. And, the better it is for Mike's life at work, with his teams, leaders, and customers.

As Mike will tell you: "Far too many people allow stress to go unmanaged, leading to bad stress. Don't be one of those people. From my story, you can see bad stress can lead to failure in all areas of your life."

For insight, here is a summary of where many businesspeople experience breakdowns from prolonged, excessive, or repetitive stress.

Why you need to unlock your stress mastery to better manage and reduce your stress:

- Makes you sick – Did you know that a vast majority of doctor visits are for stress-related illness and disease? The U.S. Federal Government and the Centers for Disease Control and Prevention report that 90% of all sickness and disease is related to stress. Stress leads to conditions including ulcers, hypertension, and mental and physical breakdowns, to mention a few.
- Dumbs you down – Stress decreases blood flow and circulation to your higher intellectual centers. This can reduce your ability to focus, form new memories, and recall others, as well as lower creativity (thinking and problem-solving skills).
- Tires you – You hear this from people under executive stress. "I am tired all the time – physically, emotionally, and mentally." This is because they do not have the right level of kinetic energy. Without this energy, your focus is weak, as is your immune system and your brilliance.
- Makes you approach everything with negativity – "I don't have much to contribute. I can't do it. I don't belong." When a person thinks like this, they eventually believe these thoughts to be the truth. But they're not; it's just the stress talking.
- Makes you fail at almost any goal or aspiration – The only logical conclusion to the points above. How can you achieve success when you're sick, dumbed-down, tired, and cynical? You may be able to push that rock uphill for a while, but eventually, it will roll back down and crush you.

In case you're wondering, yes, Mike did take action. Mike jumped into the Stress Mastery Course. Result? He is back to being Mike, hitting it out of the ballpark. His wife is grateful for the renewed intimacy, and the kids love Dad being present and fun. It's a family that lives, loves, and matters. And the company just took the award for Best In Class under Mike's leadership.

HOW TO SET YOUR FOUNDATION FOR MANAGING STRESS

First things first: your foundation. We lay down a strong foundation for you. You're going to be amazed at the speed we dig deep and reveal an abundance of information. We move with speed and accuracy using scientific rigor (implementing the highest standards and best practices of advanced scientific methods and applying evidence-based research).

It is all about discovering the truth of the best version of you (your most effective, efficient, and productive self) that amplifies results. Plus, identifying and measuring stress that is currently growing you and destroying you. Setting the foundation is simple and fast for you. Fast, as you will break away for five-to-ten-minutes to complete a ProScan® Survey. Simple, as our team of experts go to work for you immediately; experts and systems with forty years of evidence-based research and millions of case studies (PDP, Inc., 2020 Research). Your survey inputs will journey through the most innovative art, science, and technology for creating and authoring your personal story.

What is your personal story? It opens with the first chapter of you at your best, free from the harmful impacts of stress. The second chapter tells a story of both the good stress growing you and bad stress destroying you.

After you receive your personal story, you jump into an online and on-demand virtual sixty-minute training session to prepare yourself mentally, emotionally, and professionally to manage and reduce stress through the Stress Mastery Course.

What's behind the curtain of your foundation – your personal story?

Here are **two steps** for creating your foundation, where we write your personal story.

Our experts will ghostwrite your personal story for you to review and approve.

Step 1, take five-to-ten-minutes to respond to the ProScan® Survey, and we will write your personal story that includes the following chapters: Basic/Natural Self, Priority Environments, and Predictor/Outward Self.

Here is an overview of each chapter.

Basic/Natural Self

How would you like to see a chapter about you showing up at your best?

The Basic/Natural Self is the best version of you. The millions of entrepreneurs we have written their story for will tell you: "It's you at the top of your game, enjoying being your most authentic, efficient, effective, and productive self – playing to your strengths and amplifying results." And you'll love it, as stress is no longer holding you back.

You're serving and delivering higher value to others. You're in a new state of being, and you're all in, and in the flow. It's like the world is now happening for you and not to you. You connect to a vision more significant than you, that's more inclusive and selfless. Your mind has the clarity of what you want, and your heart feels it already happening. And you find yourself empowered, in love with life, free, and grateful. You're creating more value and attracting the life and wellbeing you want for yourself and others. You self-regulate your response to the outer environment. Pressures and stress are no longer limiting you. You're now living a better life fulfilling your dreams, business, health, and relationships.

Priority Environment(s)

The second chapter of your story serves to provide you with a stress analysis.

Now that you've seen yourself crushing it, it's time to see what is currently holding you back from being your best to get the results you want. This is where you are being forced externally, or feeling the need internally, to make the following adjustments, good and bad, relevant to control, influence, inspiration, timing, details, and decision-making. Plus, it shows if you're being boxed in by pressures or holding back in response to internal pressures. Or, if you're stretching beyond capacity or being required to do more than you want to in a given area. Then the chapter dives into your level of satisfaction with your life and work. Are you satisfied with your ability to create, out-innovate, launch, grow, and sustain?

Your Private Stress Analysis measures the intensities of stress that are either growing or destroying you, your level of satisfaction relevant to fulfilling what is important to you in your life and work, and the amount of remaining energy that can be used to grow and rebuild.

Predictor/Outward Self

This chapter shows how you come across to others—giving you insight into your initial behavior upon first contact, starting a business, leading a team, managing a project, collaborating on a social event, or delegating activities.

As a bonus included with the chapters, you will see a report of what truly motivates and demotivates you and the overriding needs you currently have.

Step 2, welcome to the online and on-demand virtual training. Learn how self-awareness is essential for ultimate achievement. If you don't understand what motivates your actions and behaviors, it's difficult to cultivate positive growth. On your journey toward detailing the unique strengths that drive you, it's essential to measure the limitations of stress holding you back from success. To ensure long-term sustainable success, we will measure your success formula, included but not limited to behavioral traits, decision-making, energy styles, operational styles, communication styles, leadership styles, backup styles, and motivators that propel you forward and keep you a chapter ahead. You will learn how to leverage your strengths for a life of achievement that aligns with your personal values.

The sixty-minute online and on-demand virtual training will:

- ✓ Walk you, step by step, toward discovering WHY you should spend more time in your strengths and less time in your weaknesses to achieve what matters most with focus, clarity, and energy.

- ✓ Show how your strengths will generate and attract the life you want.
- ✓ Apply precise measurements of where stress is growing or destroying what you want in life.
- ✓ Build the foundation for the Stress Mastery Course to control your response to pressures that cause stress and thus stay in control of your success and fulfillment.

LINK TO THE ONLINE AND ON-DEMAND VIRTUAL TRAINING "FOUNDATION FOR MANAGING STRESS":

https://begin2learn.com

For any issues with the link, please contact customer support found at the end of this Chapter, Chapter 3.

STRESS MASTERY COURSE

Now that you have read about and hopefully taken the virtual training to set your foundation, you're now ready to jump into the Stress Mastery Course. The Stress Mastery Course is where you will find the three keys to unlock your stress mastery.

This gold-standard three-module course helps you manage stress to achieve what you want most in life and work by using proven stress-management tools and techniques to achieve it. You will learn and grow to use stress as a force to achieve a rewarding lifestyle, reduce the stress holding you back, and remain in control of stress before it controls you. The primary aim is for you to unlock your ability to better master stress and confidently stay in control of your dreams, business, health, and relationships in ways you never thought possible.

We all want to control stress before it controls us, but most of us don't have a clue where or how to begin. The Stress Mastery Course contains concrete, easy-to-use stress-management techniques to break through the limitations of stress and create the results you desire.

Now is the time to unlock your stress mastery for growth and rebuilding.

Here's what the Stress Mastery Course will do for you:

Why take the course? To grow and rebuild your wealth, health, and relationships. I love the idea that every one of us has the opportunity to wake up every morning with purpose and operate on purpose. It doesn't matter the pressures and stress, because you are in control of how you respond to pressures and demands that cause stress. That opportunity to control our response and level up our life and work is available to all of us. Everybody has the ability to wake up inspired and successful in their life and work and end each day feeling fulfilled.

When should you take the course? Now, to stay in control of your dreams, business, health, and relationships.

How much time will I need to complete the Stress Mastery Course? It doesn't matter what your schedule is like, it's a total of six hours at your pace. For best results, plan to set aside at least two hours per week over the next three weeks to complete the three modules of the Stress Mastery Course.

Where to take the course? The course is an online and on-demand virtual learning experience. A proven learning experience that provides immediate high-value results.

Available Anytime – Lack of time is a key challenge for entrepreneurs. Leaders can access their online and on-demand virtual learning course anytime, even outside of traditional business hours.

Accessible Anywhere – Geographic limitations aren't an issue with online and on-demand virtual learning. Leaders can choose the module and connect from anywhere in the world.

Reduced Environmental Impact – Online and on-demand virtual learning eliminates travel expenses associated with traditional face-to-face and traditional classroom learning.

Group Coaching – Deepens trust and collaboration among leaders to speed up the realization of personal and professional development results.

We understand that you want to get more out of life. We also understand you are very busy and have your business, family, friends, community, and hardly any free time. We designed this three-module course so that you can work through it even if you're hard pressed for time. We have created a culture of progress inside Stress Mastery.

Learn, grow, expand, and improve at the time and cadence that works best for you. Take control of your response to pressures that cause stress to stay in control of your success and fulfillment. Use the three keys to unlock your stress mastery and live using the power of your strengths to fuel your success.

Don't allow your life to be anything less than extraordinary. Say yes to the Stress Mastery Course and begin your journey today!

LINK TO "STRESS MASTERY COURSE"

https://grow2profit.com/

For any issues with the link, please contact customer support found at the end of this Chapter, Chapter 3.

STRESS MASTERY COURSE – THE THREE KEYS TO MANAGING STRESS – UNLOCKING YOUR STRESS MASTERY

Key 1 – BE THE BEST VERSION OF YOURSELF

Join the movement of entrepreneurs gaining control of their dreams, health, companies, and relationships.

Here's Exactly What You're Going to Get With Key 1

- ✓ Module 1 of the three-module course begins with "Be the Best Version of Yourself," which makes it simple to manage stress and anxiety and prevent them from holding you back.
- ✓ Discover your unique strengths in relating to others – better relate (influence and inspire) to get along and continue to serve high value to yourself and others.

✓ Gain clarity of your unique strengths in performing, moving the needle, and leveling up – better create wealth (sustain long-term impact and profit in life and work).

✓ Discover your unique strengths to be the best version of you – better maintain health (emotionally, mentally, physically, and spiritually).

✓ Live as the best version of yourself to keep stress and anxiety from jacking up your energy, job, business, relationships, health, finances, happiness, freedom, and love for life.

✓ Conquer your business seeding, startup, launch, growth, expansion, sustainment, succession, exits, or whatever you desire. Do it better by being your authentic self (most efficient, effective, and productive) to perform extraordinarily with tasks, goals, projects, and activities vital to life and work. Enjoy a healthier, wealthier, more fulfilling, passionate, and purposeful life – whether that means learning, achieving in business, reigniting relationships, or having more confidence in creating your life.

Key 2 – KNOW WHY YOU'RE SO STRESSED & ANXIOUS

Here's Exactly What You're Going to Get With Key 2

✓ Module 2 makes it simple for you to see why pressures are causing you stress.

✓ Within five-to-ten-minutes, our instrument identifies and measures the intensities of the multiple pressures and demands you're facing, causing you both good and bad stress. Do away with the old-school trial and error of only adding more stress to yourself, where you're bombarded with questions or forced to sit down with pen and paper only to fail again at breaking down the problems that are causing you stress.

✓ Speed up determining the sources of stress by precisely identifying the people and circumstances causing the pressure. Leverage the instrument to make the complicated simple and timely. The sources of stress are many: coming from work, family, social life, economic factors, health, and beliefs – you can get to the source faster and with high accuracy so that you can immediately begin managing and reducing the limitations of stress that are holding you back from the life you want.

✓ See why your energy is being drained, not just generally, but specifically – emotionally, mentally, and physically.

✓ Understand why you currently experience the level of satisfaction you have right now, be it high, medium, or low. Quickly course-correct to experience the achievement and fulfillment you want in both life and work.

✓ See where the measures and intensities of stress can grow and destroy you. Gain focus and clarity for scalable and sustainable growth.

✓ Identify what external pressures are compressing or boxing you in, and thus preventing you from performing at your best to realize the best.

✓ Recognize where pressures are misdirecting your resources and stretching you outside of your sweet spot.

✓ Confirm what pressures inhibit your ability to think best, choose best, and act best to experience what you desire.

Key 3 – MANAGE & REDUCE STRESS BEFORE IT MANAGES & REDUCES YOU

Here's Exactly What You're Going to Get With Key 3

✓ Module 3 makes it easy to use the three best practices to manage and reduce stress and anxiety.

✓ Overcome the state of prolonged stress and anxiety.

✓ Attract an abundant life and wellbeing through a healthy relationship with God, yourself, and others.

✓ Take control to best respond to life's pressures so they don't stress you out.

✓ Create a state of abundance where you experience empowerment, freedom, love for life, and gratefulness.

✓ Grow and rebuild any area of your life and work.

✓ Leverage evidence-based research and case studies that prove that you increase your confidence, self-esteem, and worth when you control stress.

✓ Reduce stress to level up your ability to grow and rebuild.

✓ For your health, control stress to elevate your immune system (sustaining health), your work (generating wealth), and your ability to cope (relating to God, yourself, others, and life).

LINK TO "STRESS MASTERY COURSE":

https://grow2profit.com/

For any issues with the link, please contact customer support found at the end of this Chapter, Chapter 3.

For Continual Growth and Rebuilding: Private Facebook Group

✓ This closed, exclusive Facebook group is your way to instantly plug into a network of like-minded people who level up their lives and work.

✓ Exchange ideas, tips, tricks, and epiphanies to keep stress under control to stay in control.

✓ Connect with a group of people who share the same values, goals, and beliefs.

✓ Receive live group coaching to help you develop a better approach to "show up" at your best as your organization faces new pressures and challenges that cause stress.

You have read, listened, and learned about how entrepreneurs overcome stress to consistently level up, move the needle, impact, and profit as they serve massive value to their loved ones and customers.

These entrepreneurs who overcome the limitations of stress remain in control even in economic contractions or chaotic uncertain times, and simultaneously experience new personal and professional heights of extraordinary happiness and long-term success.

You might believe these entrepreneurs have some distinct advantage over you, but they don't. These entrepreneurs have used the three keys to unlock stress that leads to failure to launch, implement, grow, and sustain in every area of their life. Using the three keys to master their adjustment to pressures that cause stress is their framework for enjoying higher achievement and fulfillment.

These same keys are now available for you to take control of stress and achieve what you want in your life and business.

Be forewarned: this isn't some half-baked unproven theory. It's real-world results, proven through time-tested reliability and validity to ensure accuracy. It's actionable, measurable, trainable, repeatable, transferable, manageable, and doable for you to reduce stress to enjoy more success in your journey at any point in time.

I am excited to share this book's framework, which has provided a personal road map to higher achievement for millions of entrepreneurs and business leaders.

I believe these three keys to managing and reducing stress housed inside the foundational work and Stress Mastery Course will enable you to elevate and achieve what you never thought possible in your life and business.

Customer Support
Support: https://pdpfyns.com/customer-support/
Phone Support: 719-357-5879

ABOUT THE AUTHOR

Jim Farmer is the best-selling author of *Unlock Your Stress Mastery*.

His clients encouraged him to write this book. To no longer let stress hold you back from realizing what you want with your dreams, business, health, and relationships. To deliver a proven stress-management process that will help you compress decades into days, learn through others' experiences, eliminate trial and error, and give you a clear pathway to create the life you want.

The author isn't a business academic or consultant or reporter of theory – when it comes to rising above the clutter of stress to amplify business results during chaotic uncertain times, Jim "lives it and makes it happen." For thirty-five plus years, Jim led multiple healthcare industry companies to perform scalable, sustainable growth in sales, profits, customers as raving fans, team satisfaction, and business-owner satisfaction during economic ups and downs. The scalable, sustainable growth, especially during the pressures of uncertain times, called for keeping himself and the teams in control of stress.

Fast forward.

Through decades of employing the best practices and continual research, Jim cleaned up the theories to make them simple for entrepreneurs to adapt and thus manage the stress that inhibits growth and rebuilding.

Jim is now Co-Founder of FYNS (Find Your Natural Strengths), which brings out the entrepreneur's best version of themselves. His mission is to free every entrepreneur to be more and achieve more, by showing up as the best version of themself.